Three Cheers for Us!

HOUGHTON MIFFLIN HARCOURT
School Publishers

Contents

TEKS **1.3A** decode words in context and in isolation; **1.3D** decode words with common spelling patterns; **1.3E** read words with inflectional endings

Phonics

Words with -ed and -ing Read the lists. Tell how the base word changes when an ending is added. Then complete the sentences. Spell the word.

hop	hope	tap	tape
hopped	hoped	tapped	taped
hopping	hoping	tapping	taping

1. The frog is _____ up and down.

2. Ted _____ his ripped paper.

Bears

by Anne Miranda

What things do bears like? Just
look and see!

Bears like eating. This black bear is sitting up in a tree. It is getting nuts. It grabbed them and ate them. It likes eating nuts!

Bears like fishing. Fishing is best
when streams are filled with fish.
Fast swimming fish race past this
bear. They are racing up stream.

Bears like swimming. It is a thrill
to see this big, white bear swimming
in the sea! It is bobbing up and
down in the waves like floating ice.
It swims toward the ice.

This bear has an itch. He likes scratching. He is rubbing his back on that tree. He looks as if he is grinning. He must have found just the spot to scratch.

This bear likes napping. It can
sleep well even during the day. It will
wake up and go trotting off to look
for food. It will eat and nap again.
This bear likes napping a lot.

This bear likes digging. It has
been digging a den. It will line its
den with branches and grass. Grass
makes a soft mattress. It will be a
nice bed to nap in.

This bear likes sleeping at night with the moon shining above. It stretched and nodded off. Sleep well, bear! Sleep well!

TEKS 1.14B identify important facts/details; **ELPS 1C** use strategic learning techniques to acquire vocabulary

Facts

Identify Important Facts

Reread the story "Bears" with a partner. Then share the important facts you learned with your partner.

Draw and Write Draw and label a picture to show what you learned.

Phonics

Words with -ed and -ing Read the story. Then reread each underlined word. Name the base word and the ending. Tell how the base word changed.

Ray hopped up and waved a flag. The kids were racing. Max tripped and stopped running. Carl was jogging fast. Carl hoped to win, but Jan raced by him. Jan smiled and said, "Winning is fun!"

Hiding and Seeking

by Lance Langley

illustrated by Dominic Catalano

The kits liked their first grade
teacher, Miss Fox. Miss Fox liked
them, and she liked playing games.
She was fun!

At playtime, the kits begged for
a game of Hide and Seek. Miss Fox
was IT. Miss Fox counted to ten.
Her class hid while she counted.

Red was hiding in a good place,
but he did not sit still. He wagged
his tail. Miss Fox spotted Red. She
tagged him. Red was out.

Meg was hiding in this very good place, but her ears jutted out. Miss Fox spotted Meg. She tagged her. Meg was out.

Blaze was hiding in a good place,
but he clapped and hummed. Miss
Fox spotted Blaze. She tagged him.
Blaze was out.

Jill was hiding in a good place.
She hid in a tree above Miss Fox.
Miss Fox looked and looked but she
didn't see Jill. Jill smiled.

Miss Fox hunted up and down for
Jill. Jill had fun fooling Miss Fox.
Jill's laughs made Jill's tree shake.
Miss Fox saw it shaking.

Miss Fox spotted Jill at last! Miss
Fox tagged her. Jill was out. Jill
was good at hiding, but Miss Fox was
great at seeking!

TEKS **1.3H** identify/read high-frequency words; **1.3I** monitor decoding accuracy; **1.5** read aloud with fluency/comprehension; **ELPS 4A** learn English sound-letter relationships/decode

Fluency

Words to Know   You have to remember some words. Read these words.

above	teacher	laughs
great	very	was

Read Aloud   Work with a partner. Take turns reading aloud "Hiding and Seeking." Help each other read words correctly.

Phonics

Long e Spelled y and ie Read the words. What letters stand for long e?

field   piece   shield   chief   niece

Read these word pairs. What letter or letters stand for long e? How many syllables does each word have?

story	copy	study
stories	copied	studies
hurry	bunny	
hurried	bunnies	

Speedy and Chase

by Christopher K. Lyne

illustrated by Rick Stromoski

It was sunny but not too hot. It was a good day for a race. Goats, pigs, and cows lined up in the field. They would get a good look.

Chase looked at Speedy. Chase studied him. Speedy hopped in place. Chase hoped he could keep up with Speedy. Was Speedy as speedy as he looked?

"I plan on winning this race!" shouted Speedy.

"You seem fast," said Chase.

"Yes!" Speedy grinned. "Fast and planning on winning. It will be easy!"

"Get ready. Go!" yelled Sheep.
Speedy zoomed past clapping
fans. Speedy really was speedy!
Chase jogged past them at his own
slow pace.

Speedy took the lead. "Chase can't catch up," Speedy bragged. "I feel a bit sleepy. I will win even if I take a nap!"

He flopped down and napped.

Speedy was still napping when
Chase jogged by. He was running at
his own slow pace. He was smiling,
too.

Chase pushed on toward the finish
line. Chase didn't give up. He kept
on going. Fans clapped and yelled.
Speedy woke up surprised!

Speedy had planned on winning,
but Chase was first. Chase was the
winner!

Kinds of Books

Read Together

Nonfiction or Fantasy If a story gives information about real animals, it is nonfiction. If the animals in a story do things that no real animals can do, the story is fantasy.

Write Work with a partner. Decide if "Speedy and Chase" is nonfiction or fantasy. Write reasons why you think so.

Phonics

Words with -er and -est Read the words. Tell how base words change when -er or -est is added.

smart	nice	thin	happy
smart**er**	nic**er**	thin**ner**	happ**ier**
smart**est**	nic**est**	thin**nest**	happ**iest**

Use words in the lists and other words to complete these sentence starters.

1. My pet _____.

2. In school, _____.

The Three Races

by Madeleine Jeffries

illustrated by Amanda Harvey

Fran had her box of cars. She
and Ken each chose two racecars.

Ken picked a slick red racecar.
Fran picked next. She chose a much
bigger blue car. Fran hoped it was
faster, too. Speedier cars win!

Then Ken picked a racecar with black stripes. Fran picked next. Fran picked a green car. It was nicer and had fatter wheels than Ken's.

In the first race, Fran's bigger
blue car raced Ken's slick red car.
Ken and Fran lined them up at the
top of the hill.

Fran's car zipped faster than
Ken's. Ken's car was much slower.
Fran's car raced fast enough to win.
That made Fran happy.

In the next race, Ken's striped car raced Fran's green car. This time, Ken's car zoomed faster. It was fast enough to win. It made Ken happy.

Ken and Fran had one last race. Fran's speedy blue car raced Ken's fast striped car.

Which car would be faster?

The cars raced at the same speed.
Fran's car was not faster. Ken's car
was not faster. That made Fran and
Ken happy, too!

Decoding

Read
Together

Read Carefully   Read the story.

My car has four fat wheels and thin stripes. It is slower than Fran's car. Fran's car is bigger than mine, too. But I made my car by myself, so I like it a lot.

Think   If a word is hard to read, use the sounds of the letters to figure it out. Also, remember if it looks like a word you have learned. Reread the story.

TEKS **1.3A** decode words in context and in isolation; **1.3D** decode words with common spelling patterns; **1.3E** read words with inflectional endings

Phonics

Words with -er, -est Read each word pair. Tell how the base words change when -er or -est is added.

big - bigger   late - later

new - newest   cloudy - cloudiest

Read the sentences. Name the base word and ending in the underlined words.

1. Jenny's hat is the <u>flattest</u>.

2. Don's hat is <u>funnier</u> than Jenny's.

3. Ellen's hat is the <u>finest</u> of all.

Seed Sisters

by Anne Miranda

illustrated by Janet Pedersen

It is spring. Liz and Rose are shopping for seeds. Liz and Rose always plant seeds in the spring.

Rose picks a smaller pack of
seeds. Liz's pack is much bigger.
Liz and Rose go back home to plant
the seeds that they just got.

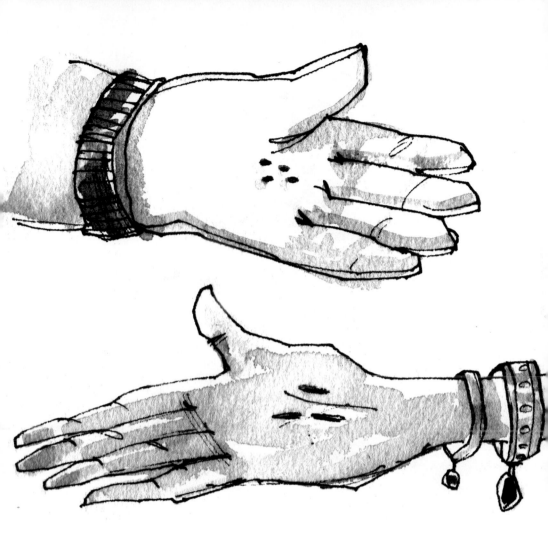

Liz and Rose see that the seeds in each pack are different. Rose's seeds are much smaller and rounder. Liz's seeds are much longer and flatter.

Liz and Rose dig. Liz digs faster than Rose. Liz plants her seeds first. Rose digs slower than Liz. Rose plants her seeds last.

The seeds sprout. Liz's seeds
sprout quicker. Rose's seeds are
slower to sprout. Liz and Rose rake
and weed their backyard plot once.

47

All spring the plants grow. They
grow bigger and bigger and bigger
each day. Liz's plants are different
from Rose's.

Liz's plants grow higher than
Rose's plants. Rose's are shorter.
Rose and Liz tell stories as they
wait for the plant buds to open!

The plants are in bloom. How
nice the backyard looks! Rose and
Liz think their yard is the nicest yard
in town!

Vocabulary

Read
Together

Action Words   Read the verbs.

| plant   dig   rake   weed   grow |

Act It Out   Work with
a partner. Read the verbs
together. Then write each
word on a card. Place the
cards face-down. Pick a card
and act out the word. Can
your partner can guess the
word? Then have your partner
act out a word and you guess
the action.

TEKS **1.3A** decode words in context and in isolation; **1.3C(iii)** decode using final stable syllables; **1.3C(vi)** decode using r-controlled vowel pattern

Phonics

Words with Two Syllables

Read. Listen for two syllables.

apple puddle simple jingle

Read each sentence and tell which picture it matches.

1. Ed's shirt is purple.

2. My dog is a poodle.

3. Jokes make me giggle.

Jingle, Jangle, and Jiggle

by Jose Pitkin

illustrated by Judy Stead

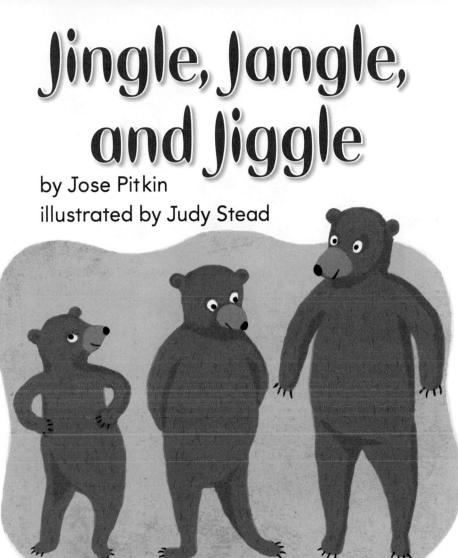

Jingle, Jangle, and Jiggle are
pals. Jingle is the shortest. Jiggle is
the biggest. Jangle is in the middle.

Jingle, Jangle, and Jiggle are clowns. Clowns make us chuckle and giggle. They always dress in funny hats and pants. They put on funny noses.

Jiggle has the longest nose. It
makes a loud honking sound. Now it
is missing! Where can it be? It is a
puzzle. Jiggle must get it back!

Jiggle looks inside Jangle's boots.
He looks inside Jingle's hat. Jiggle
does not see his nose. He starts
to grumble.

Jiggle looks in high places. Jingle
looks in low places. Silly Jangle looks
in a popcorn box! Jiggle's nose is still
missing.

Jiggle sobs and sniffles. "I need
my nose," he mumbles. Then a
blue bird comes near. Jiggle's nose
dangles from the bird's beak!

58

Jiggle jumps up. The bird zooms high. Jiggle cannot catch it. Then the bird dips low. Jiggle tackles that bird. He snatches his nose back!

Jiggle puts on his nose. He gives
it the biggest, loudest, silliest honk he
can! Then Jingle, Jangle, and Jiggle
take a bow.

TEKS 1.1F Identify information provided by book parts; **ELPS** 1C use strategic learning techniques to acquire vocabulary

Book Information

Read Together

Illustrators An **illustrator** creates pictures for stories. Point to the illustrator's name.

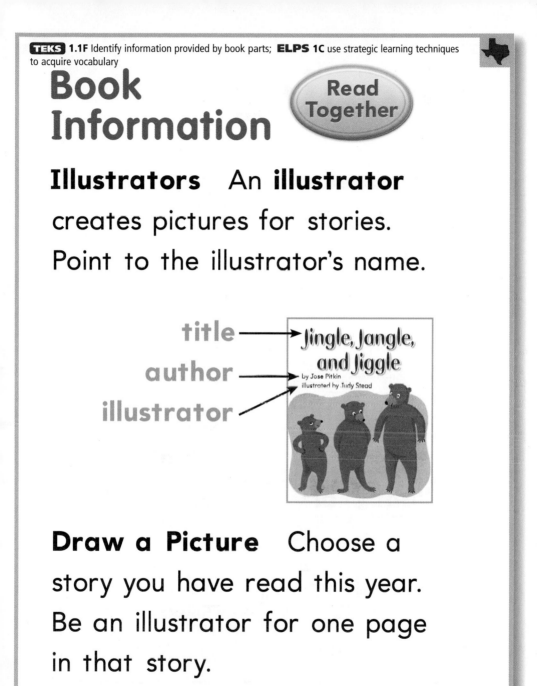

title → Jingle, Jangle, and Jiggle

author → by Jose Pitkin

illustrator → illustrated by Judy Stead

Draw a Picture Choose a story you have read this year. Be an illustrator for one page in that story.

61

Phonics

Long i Spelled igh, y, ie Read each word. Tell which letter or letters stand for long i. Use two words in a sentence.

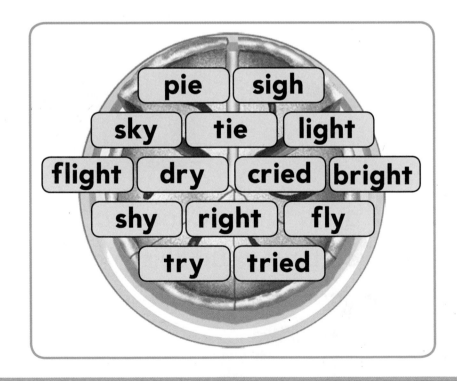

pie sigh
sky tie light
flight dry cried bright
shy right fly
try tried

Sally Jane and Beth Ann

by James McKinley
illustrated by Tom Leonard

Sally Jane was a large brown bat.
She spent much of her time hanging
by her feet in her safe, dark cave.

At night, Sally Jane liked to
fly across the sky. She could hear
sounds from far away. Her good
hearing helped her catch bugs.

Last night, Sally Jane heard an
odd sound. She saw a bat that
needed help. It was Beth Ann.

"My wing is snagged in this net,"
Beth Ann cried.

"I will try to get you out," Sally
Jane said with a bright smile.

Sally Jane gave it her best try.
She tugged and bit at the net. At
last, Beth Ann got free!

"Let's fly," said Sally Jane.

"I can't fly," groaned Beth Ann.
"My wing is still stiff."

"My, my, so it is," sighed Sally
Jane. "Let me try to pick you up. I
can fly you back to my cave."

"You can lift me!" cried Beth Ann.
"I am strong," boasted Sally Jane.
"Let's go then!" said Beth Ann.
Sally Jane held Beth Ann tight
and took flight.

Sally Jane flew high across the
sky. Beth Ann was in her grasp. They
landed in the cave. Beth Ann thanked
Sally Jane. Sally Jane was happy to
help her new buddy, Beth Ann.

TEKS 1.9B describe/analyze characters; **RC-1(D)** make inferences/use textual evidence; **ELPS** 4G demonstrate comprehension through shared reading/retelling/responding/note-taking

Characters

Read Together

Answer Questions Think about the story "Sally Jane and Beth Ann." Answer these questions with a partner.

- How did Sally Jane feel when she heard an odd sound?
- How did Beth Ann feel when she was snagged in a net?
- How do you think Sally Jane and Beth Ann felt when they got back to the cave?

Phonics

Long i Spelled igh, y, ie Read each clue. Tell which picture matches the clue. Reread the long **i** words.

1. Use this to shine bright light.

2. Use this to tie a tight knot.

3. Use this to stay dry.

4. Use this to look at the night sky.

Ty and Big Gilly

by Carson Fisher

illustrated by John Wallner

Ty had a hobby that made him happy. His hobby was fishing. Ty liked fishing.

Ty had a large fishing box. He
kept it right by his bed. It was filled
with hooks, jelly bugs, and all sorts
of fishing stuff. It also had a fly that
his dad had made.

One bright, sunny day, Ty and his
dad went fishing. Ty had his fishing
box, rod, and reel. He and Dad
hiked to Sand Lake.

Ty sat under the pale blue sky as
he baited his hook. He used a jelly
bug. Ty closed his fishing box lid. Ty
tried to keep the box neat and clean.

Ty threw back his line. He let it
fly high across the lake. His jelly bug
landed with a plop! Dad cast his
line. Ty and Dad waited.

Then Ty had a bite! Ty had to reel it in. He gave it his best try. The fish was fighting hard. Then the fish on his line jumped up and out of the water. It was big!

It jumped a second time. What a
sight! It was Big Gilly! Big Gilly had
a big head. Its tail snapped back
and forth. "That's the biggest fish in
Sand Lake," Dad cried out.

Ty grabbed Big Gilly and took out
the hook. He let Big Gilly go. Big
Gilly swam off, still king of Sand Lake.
Dad winked at Ty. He was glad Ty
let Big Gilly go.

Vocabulary

Read Together

Plural Nouns Read the sentences. Write them on a sheet of paper.

- Ty and his dad went fishing.
- Ty's box was full of hooks and jelly bugs.
- Dad brought fishing rods.
- Ty's jelly bug landed in the lake.

Underline the nouns that name one. Circle the nouns that name more than one.

Phonics

Base Words and Endings Read each sentence. Reread each underlined word. Name the base word and the ending.

1. Ed <u>likes</u> <u>reading</u> the <u>funnies</u>.

2. The <u>boxes</u> are <u>filled</u> with <u>toys</u>.

3. Barb is the ice <u>skating</u> <u>winner</u>!

Benches

by Jillian Raymundo
illustrated by Elizabeth Sayles

Benches! Benches! Benches! See
them in cities. See them in towns.
See them in parks. See them at
beaches. Benches! Benches!

83

Benches are like outside couches.
They are good places to sit. Kids
sit on benches in yards and parks.
Buddies can sit side by side and chat.

Dogs and puppies go out on
leashes. Grown-ups, kids, and pets
sit on benches. Benches are good for
sitting and resting.

Kids eat lunch on benches.
Many kids have lunchboxes. When
lunchtime is over the kids might sit
and rest on benches. Then they
might play ball or jump rope.

Kids read books on benches. Kids read the funnies and comics, too. Kids read on benches when it is sunny and bright. When it rains, benches are not good places for reading.

Kids play games on benches.
Some kids are winners. Some kids
don't win. Still, kids like playing
games outside.

Moms, dads, and kids sit on benches at beaches. This dad likes to watch the sea flow in and out. What a sight!

Benches for you and benches for me,
on city streets or at the sea!
I should sit and you should, too,
on benches at parks or at the zoo!

Use Strategies

Read Together

Read for Understanding Reread **Benches** on pages 83–90 carefully.

Correct and Adjust As you read the selection, you might not understand a part of it. Do one or more of these things to help you:

- Reread it aloud.
- Picture in your mind what it is about.
- Think about what you already know, such as a time when you have sat on a bench.
- Ask yourself a question about the meaning, such as **Why is the bench a good place to sit?**

Phonics

Suffixes -y, -ly, -ful Read each word. Find three words in a row that end with the same suffix.

speedy	helpful	loudly
quickly	useful	sadly
shyly	joyful	peppery

Quiz Game

by Cindy Wahl

Hello! This book has a quick quiz
on each page. I'm hopeful that you'll
like this book. I like it a lot.

Which animal can sing sweetly?
Which can purr softly? Which can
growl loudly? Which can make
a squeaky sound?

Which animal can zip by quickly?
Which will go by slowly? Which can
wiggle by in a zigzag path? Which
can go by in a leap?

Which animal has long, helpful claws? Which has a big hump? Which can be stinky? Which looks spotty?

Which fish looks like a snake?
Which has three white stripes? Which
has five black stripes? Which has
more than six legs?

Which animal has a shell? Which animals are furry? Which is a dog? Which is a cat? Which is the biggest?

Which bird can fly? Which can
swim in icy water? Which has bright
feathers? Which has long legs?

Did you like this quick quiz? Was it fun? Do you have any ideas for a new quiz?

Write

Questions   Write facts about the animals in "Quiz Game."   Turn the facts into quiz questions.   Check that nouns and verbs are in the correct order, like these.

Fact	**Question**
A giraffe is tall.	Is a giraffe tall?
A pig has four legs.	How many legs does a pig have?

Take turns with a partner asking your questions.   Find the answers.

Phonics

Suffixes -y, -ly, -ful Read the paragraph. Find and copy words that end with each suffix. Read the words.

"I'm thankful that you stopped," Lee said shyly. "You were helpful. My helmet was useful. From now on, I'll skate more slowly. I'll look out for bumpy spots, too."

Jack and the Beans

by Anthony Swede
illustrated by Holli Conger

Jack and Jill had a big plot of land and a nice fat cow, but Jack and Jill did not have much food. Jack and Jill ate their last handful of oatmeal.

Jack had an idea. He took his
nice fat cow to town. He could sell his
cow and get food.

Jack was gone a long, long time.
Jill did not feel happy.

At last, Jack came back with a
bagful of beans. Jack looked joyful.
He felt hopeful, but Jill was still
upset. Jack had traded his nice fat
cow for that bagful of silly beans!

That bagful of beans could not feed them for long. Then Jill heard Jack's idea. Jill liked it a lot. She gladly helped Jack with his plan.

Jack and Jill quickly got spades
and rakes. Jack and Jill dug up some
rows on their plot of land. Jack and
Jill planted Jack's beans in long rows.

Then Jack and Jill went down the hill to fetch a pail of water. Jack and Jill drenched the dry black soil one cupful at a time. Jack and Jill waited hopefully.

Soon, the beans sprouted. Jack
and Jill were happy to see those
green sprouts in that black soil. They
felt hopeful as those bean plants
grew and grew and grew.

Jack and Jill picked bagful after
bagful of beans. Those beans would
last them a long, long time. Jack
and Jill were thankful that Jack had
such a good idea.

TEKS 1.1A recognize that print represents speech; **RC-1(E)** retell/act out important story events; **ELPS** 4G demonstrate comphrehension through shared reading/retelling/responding/note-taking

Words in Print

Read Together

Dialogue Print can show what people say. Read these sentences with a partner.

> **Jack:** "Look, Jill. I got a bagful of beans!"
>
> **Jill:** "You traded our cow for beans? I am not hopeful."
>
> **Jack:** "I'm hopeful. Let's plant them. They might sprout!"

Now act it out.

Phonics

Long Vowels <u>a</u>, <u>e</u>, <u>i</u>, <u>o</u>, <u>u</u> Read each word. Tell the vowel sound and its spelling. Find three words in a row that have the long <u>e</u> sound spelled <u>e</u>.

hi	go	we
yo-yo	flu	she
find	table	me

Stew for Peg

by Frank Fenn

illustrated by Laurie Hamilton

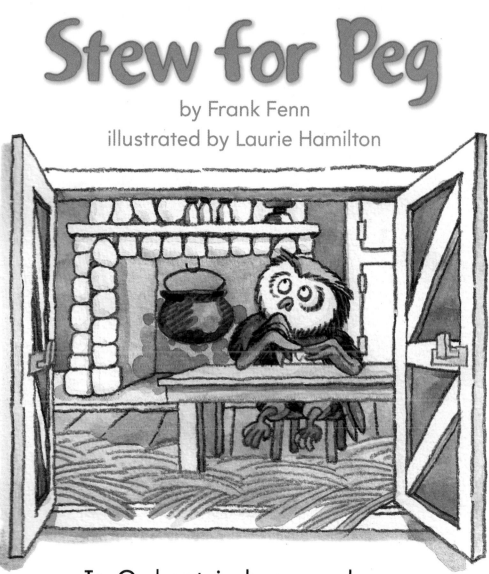

Jo Owl sat in her cozy home.
It was Peg Pig's birthday. Jo wanted
to make a treat for Peg.

"Peg likes stew," hooted Jo. "I will make a big pot of stew for Peg."

Jo was not able to make stew on her own. She didn't know how. She put a big pot of water in her cart. She went to ask for help.

Toby was helpful. He put a cupful
of red stuff in the pot.

"This will make Peg's stew really
yummy," Toby quacked loudly.

"Thanks, Toby!" hooted Jo.

Lulu was helpful. She put a
handful of green leaves in the pot.

"This will make Peg's stew really
yummy," Lulu chattered quickly.

"Thanks, Lulu!" hooted Jo.

Jo went back home. Hugo happened to be there.

"Hi," said Hugo. "What is in that pot?"

"It's really yummy stew for Peg," hooted Jo.

"Is it hot?" asked Hugo.
"Really yummy stew must be hot."
Hugo helped Jo heat it up.
"Thanks, Hugo!" hooted Jo.
"This stew smells yummy!"

118

Jo went to Peg's with her stew.

"What a treat!" squealed Peg.
"How did you make such yummy
stew, Jo?"

"I had some help," hooted Jo.

"Thank you! Thank you all!"
squealed happy Peg. "What a
yummy stew this is!"

TEKS **1.10** distinguish true stories from fantasies; **1.19C** write brief comments on texts; **ELPS** 4K employ analytical skills to demonstrate comprehension

Kinds of Books

Read Together

Nonfiction or Fantasy If a story gives facts about real animals, it is nonfiction. If the animals do things that no real animals can do, the story is fantasy.

Write Work with a partner. Decide if "Stew for Peg" is nonfiction or fantasy. Write reasons why you think so.

TEKS 1.3A decode words in isolation; **1.3C(i)** decode using closed syllables; **1.3C(ii)** decode using open syllables; **1.3C(iii)** decode using final stable syllables

Phonics

Words with Two Syllables

Read each row of words. Reread the words and clap for each syllable.

1. baby   over   moment

2. cocoa   tiger   humid

3. zero   decide   maple

4. cozy   peanut   beyond

Amy Ant

by Denise Dinkleman

illustrated by Jon Goodell

Amy Ant wakes up. It has been a long, sleepy winter. Now winter is over. It is time to leave her cozy bed.

Amy makes her way up to the field. It is sunny. How good that sunshine feels! Spring has come at last.

Flowers are blooming. Amy
decides to pick some. She sniffs the
roses. She loves that smell the most.
It reminds her of sunny days.

When her backpack is full, Amy
returns home. The sweet smell of
roses fills each room. Amy is so
happy she hums a tune. Soon music
fills each room, too.

One day, Amy sees a blue flower.
She did not see it before. She crawls
up for a better look. Amy slips!
Down, down, she slides. She is not
able to get out.

Amy shouts for help. A flying
mantis hears her. He flies into the
flower and saves Amy!

Amy thanks him and thanks him!
He tells her that his name is Rupert.

"You're as brave as a tiger!" Amy
tells him.

After that, Amy and Rupert meet
every day. They take walks and look
at flowers. They talk and have fun.

Summer is ending. Winter will
soon be on its way. Amy has to go
back down into her home. She waves
at Rupert. She is not sad. She will
see him in the sunshine next spring!

TEKS **1.3F** identify/read compound words; **1.6B** determine meaning of compound words; **ELPS 1F** use accessible language to learn new language

Compound Words

Read Together

Remember Compound words are words that are made up of two smaller words.

sand + box = sandbox

Reread Read "Amy Ant" with a partner. Take turns reading each page. When you find a compound word, raise your hand. Tell what the compound word means. Use the small words to help you.

131

TEKS **1.3A** decode words in context and in isolation; **1.3C(i)** decode using closed syllables; **1.3C(ii)** decode using open syllables; **1.3C(iii)** decode using final stable syllables

Phonics

Words with Two Syllables

Read each clue. Tell which picture it matches. Point to and reread the two-syllable words.

1. It goes with a table.

2. It can make music.

3. It is made by a spider.

4. It can go over a baby.

Julie and Jason

by Mason Sciele
illustrated by France Brassard

Julie has a pet rabbit named
Jason. Jason has black and white
fur. He sleeps in a cozy rabbit hutch
on Julie's back porch. Julie got Jason
when he was a baby.

Julie feeds Jason rabbit pellets
and hay. Jason likes his dinner. He
can sit up and behave like a dog.
After he eats, Jason can behave like
a cat. He curls up on Julie's lap.

Each day, Julie takes Jason out of
his hutch. Jason likes to play "Hide
and Seek." Jason hides and Julie
seeks. Jason sits still and silent as
Julie hunts for him.

One day, Julie's brothers took
Jason with them on a picnic. They
did not see Jason hop off beyond the
picnic table.

It was time for Julie to play with
Jason. Jason was not in his hutch or
on the porch. Julie looked all over
the house. She even looked behind
the drapes. Julie was upset. She
couldn't believe Jason was missing!

Julie asked her brothers if they
had seen Jason. Julie's brothers were
sorry they had let Jason hop away.
Then everyone looked for Jason
outside.

No one was able to find Jason.
Julie was sad. Then she had an idea.
Was Jason playing "Hide and Seek"?
She looked in places Jason had
hidden before.

Julie spotted Jason by a big
plant. She smiled. Jason saw Julie
and hopped out. Julie was so happy!
Her brothers were happy, too.

Characters

Read Together

Discuss Talk with a partner. Tell why you think the characters from **Julie and Jason** acted as they did.

Julie   Jason   Julie's brothers

Ask Questions Think about what more you want to know and understand about the characters. Take turns asking questions. Reread **Julie and Jason** on pages 133–140 and look at the pictures to find the answers.

Phonics

Prefixes <u>un-</u>, <u>re-</u> Read each word in the box. Tell what the prefix is. Then write the word that completes each sentence.

repaint rewrite unhappy untie

1. Can you _____ this knot?

2. We will _____ our stories.

3. I felt _____, but I did not cry.

4. It's time to _____ my fence.

Soccer

by Tia Yushi

illustrated by Linda Solovic

Many people believe soccer
is the best sport. Most boys and
girls play soccer.

Each player is dressed for soccer.
This coach and everyone on his team
have the same kind of shirt. This
team chose red shirts with dots. This
is the red team.

This coach and her team decided
on stripes. This is the blue team.
Their shirts look unlike the red team's
shirts. These players are putting on
long socks over shin pads.

Soccer teams need good skills. At first, team players may be unskilled at using only their feet on the field. The more teams play, the more skillful players get.

Soccer is a fast game. Soccer teams must behave safely. It is unsafe and unkind to bump into players. It is a coach's job to teach and remind players to play safely.

Each team's job is to score goals.
Blue team players try to kick the ball
into the red team's goal. Each team
has a goalkeeper. The red team's
goalkeeper tries to stop the blue
team's players from making goals.

A goalkeeper is the only player
who can pick up the ball. He or she
can catch it and keep it out of the
goal. Goalkeepers must react fast
and stop goals.

When the game ends, players say
"Good job!" no matter who wins.
Kids have fun replaying soccer games
by telling and retelling plays their
team made.

TEKS **1.14B** Identify important facts/details; **1.17E** publish/share writing; **1.19C** write brief comments on texts; **ELPS 5B** write using new basic/content-based vocabulary

Details

Read Together

Find Reread "Soccer" with a partner. Look at the pictures. List important details about playing soccer.

Soccer players wear shin pads.

Write Together, decide if you would like to play soccer. Write to explain why or why not. Share your work.

TEKS 1.3A decode words in isolation; **1.3C(v)** decode using vowel digraph/diphthong patterns; **1.3E** read words with inflectional endings; **ELPS** 2B recognize elements of English sound system;

Phonics

Read to Review   Use what you know about sounds and letters to read the words.

Long <u>e</u>: <u>ie</u>

field	chief	thief	piece
niece	shield	yield	stories
babies	ladies	hurried	studied

Long <u>i</u>: <u>y</u>

by	my	fly	dry
try	cry	sky	fry
sly	spy	shy	why

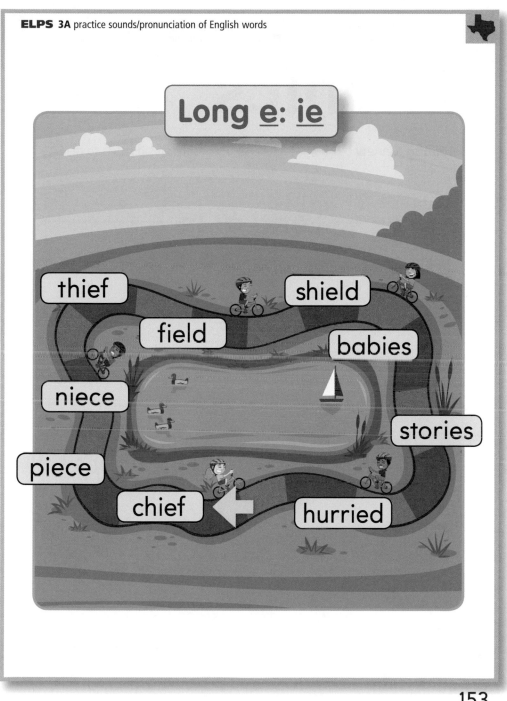

Long e: ie

thief

shield

field

babies

niece

stories

piece

chief

hurried

TEKS 1.3A decode words in isolation; **1.3C(v)** decode using vowel digraph/diphthong patterns; **1.3E** read words with inflectional endings; **ELPS 2B** recognize elements of English sound system;

Phonics

Read to Review   Use what you know about sounds and letters to read the words

Long e̲: ie̲

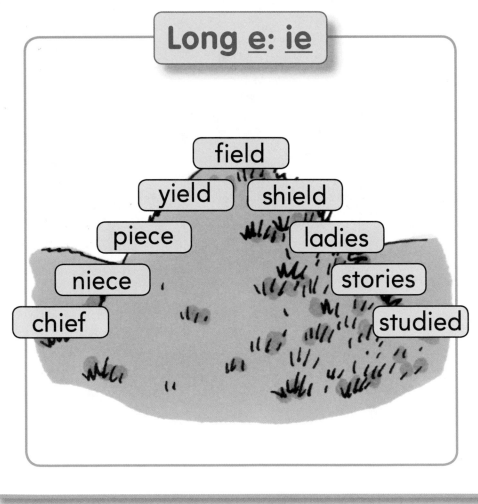

field

yield   shield

piece   ladies

niece   stories

chief   studied

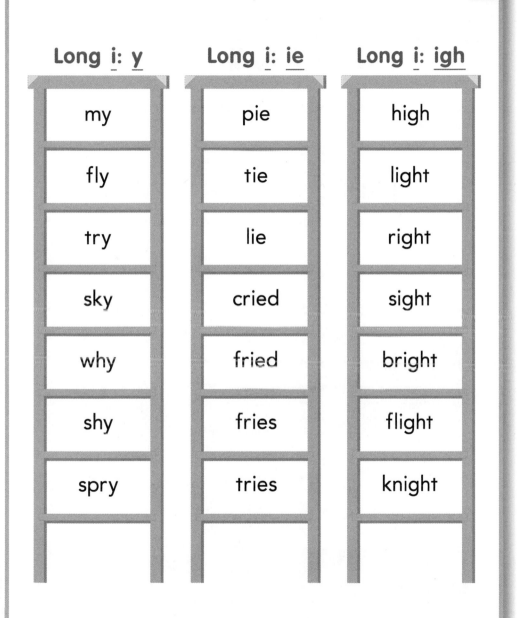

Long i: y

- my
- fly
- try
- sky
- why
- shy
- spry

Long i: ie

- pie
- tie
- lie
- cried
- fried
- fries
- tries

Long i: igh

- high
- light
- right
- sight
- bright
- flight
- knight

TEKS **1.3A** decode words in isolation; **1.3B** apply letter-sound knowledge to create words; **1.3C(v)** decode using vowel digraph/diphthong patterns; **1.3D** decode words with common spelling patterns;

Phonics

Read to Review   Use what you know about sounds and letters to read the words.

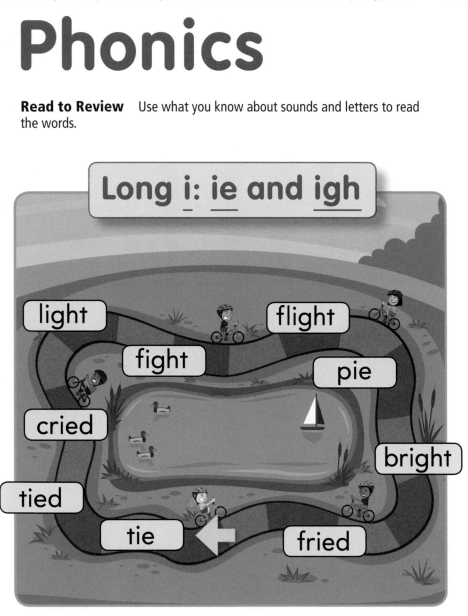

Long i: ie and igh

light

flight

fight

pie

cried

tied

bright

tie

fried

Build and Read Words   Put the letters together to read the words.
Think of more words to add.

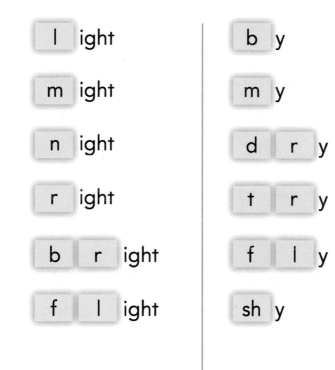

l	ight		b	y
m	ight		m	y
n	ight		d r	y
r	ight		t r	y
b r	ight		f l	y
f l	ight		sh	y

Phonics

Decode Words in Isolation   Use what you know about sounds and letters to read each word by itself.

Long e: y			
lazy	hurry	pony	happy
Tony	baby	cozy	wooly
rusty	city	nosy	bony

Words with -ed, -ing		
copied	hurried	studied
hoping	tapping	going
tried	looking	prized

TEKS 1.3A(i) decode words with consonants; **1.3A(ii)** decode words with vowels; **1.3A(iv)** decode words with consonant digraphs

Phonics

Decode Words in Isolation   Use what you know about letters and sounds to read each word by itself.

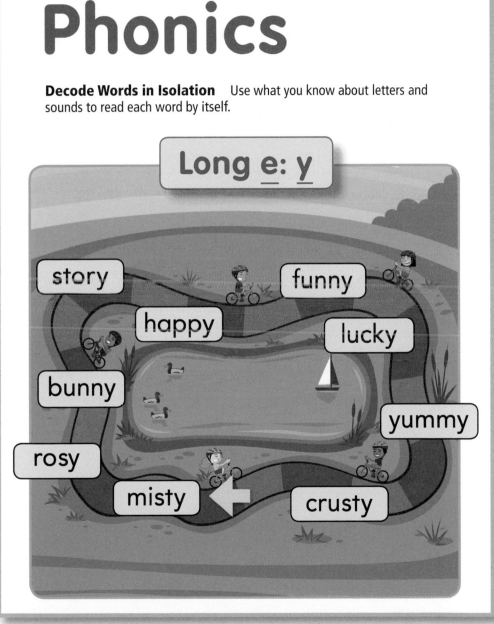

Long e̲: y̲

story

funny

happy

lucky

bunny

yummy

rosy

misty

crusty

TEKS **1.3A(i)** decode words with consonants; **1.3A(ii)** decode words with vowels; **1.3E** read words with inflectional endings

Phonics

Decode Words in Isolation   Use what you know about sounds and letters to read each word by itself.

Words with <u>le</u>

apple	table	wobble	shuttle
jiggle	ripple	purple	title
cattle	bottle	saddle	able

Long <u>e</u>: <u>y</u>

minty	happy	gusty	copy
pony	nosy	funny	silly
crusty	party	story	rosy

TEKS **1.3A(i)** decode words with consonants; **1.3A(ii)** decode words with vowels; **1.3A(iv)** decode words with consonant digraphs

Phonics

Decode Words in Isolation   Use what you know about sounds and letters to read each word by itself.

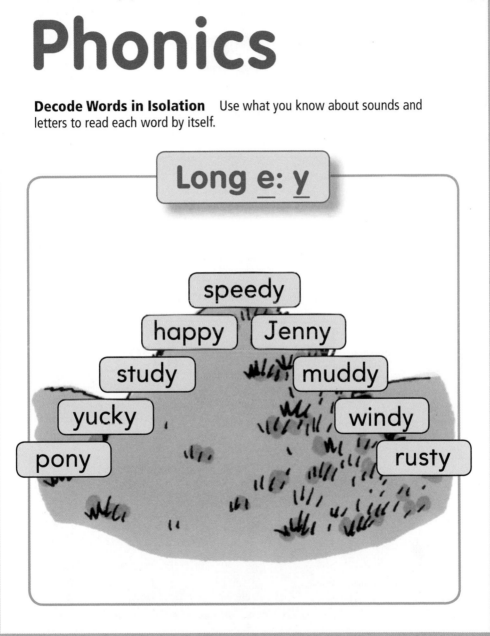

Long <u>e</u>: <u>y</u>

speedy

happy   Jenny

study   muddy

yucky   windy

pony   rusty

TEKS **1.3A(i)** decode words with consonants; **1.3A(ii)** decode words with vowels; **1.3A(iv)** decode words with consonant digraphs; **1.3A(v)** decode words with vowel digraphs

Phonics

Decode Words in Isolation   Use what you know about letters and sounds to read each word by itself.

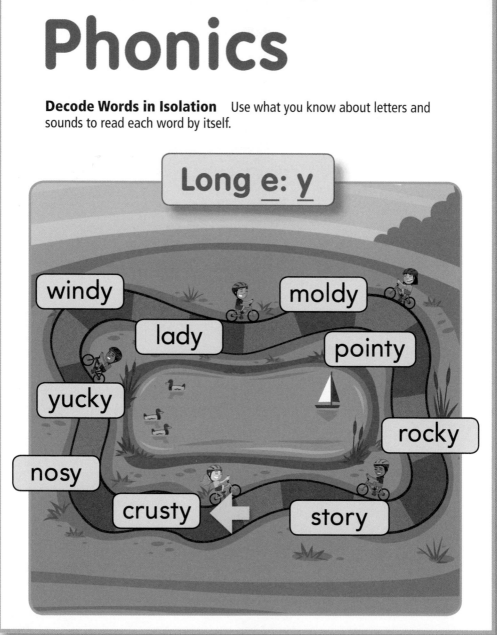

162

Word Lists

Accompanies *"The Dot"*

Bears

Decodable Words

Target Skill: Inflections *-ed, -ing* (CVC*e*, CVC)

bobbing, digging, getting, grabbed, grinning, napping, racing, rubbing, sitting, shining, swimming, trotting

Previously Taught Skills

an, and, as, at, ate, back, be, bed, best, big, black, branches, can, day, den, down, during, eat, eating, fast, filled, fish, fishing, floating, food, for, found, go, grass, grunted, has, he, his, ice, if, in, is, it, itch, just, like, likes, line, look, looks, lot, makes, mattress, moon, must, nap, nice, nuts, off, on, past, race, rubbing, sea, scratch, scratching, see, sleep, sleeping, soft, spot, stream, streams, stretched, swims, that, this, them, things, thrill, tree, up, wake, waves, well, when, white, will, with

High-Frequency Words

New

above, bear, bears, even, toward

Previously Taught

a, again, are, been, do, have, night, the, they, to

Hiding and Seeking

Decodable Words
Target Skill: Inflections *-ed, -ing* (CVC*e*, CVC)

begged, clapped, hiding, hummed jutted, liked, shaking, smiled, spotted, tagged, wagged

Previously Taught Skills
and, at, Blaze, but, class, counted, did, didn't, down, ears, first, fooling, for, Fox, fun, game, games, good, grade, had, he, her, hid, hide, him, his, hunted, in, it, Jill, Jill's, kits, last, looked, made, Meg, Miss, not, out, place, playing, playtime, Red, saw, see, seek, seeking, shake, she, sit, still, tail, ten, them, this, tree, up, while

High-Frequency Words
New
above, teacher

Previously Taught
a, great, laughs, the, their, to, very, was

Speedy and Chase

page 22

Decodable Words

Target Skill: Long e Patterns *y*, *ie*
easy, field, ready, really, sleepy, Speedy, studied, sunny

Target Skill: Inflections *-ed*, *-ing* (CVCe, CVC)
bragged, clapped, clapping, flopped, grinned, hoped, hopped, jogged, lined, napped, napping, planned, planning, running, smiling, winning

Previously Taught Skills
and, as, at, be, bit, bragged, but, can't, catch, Chase, cows, day, didn't, down, fans, fast, feel, finish, first, for, get, go, goats, going, good, had, he, him, his, hot, if, in, it, keep, kept, lead, line, look, looked, nap, not, on, own, pace, past, pigs, plan, race, seem, set, Sheep, shouted, slow, still, take, them, this, too, took, up, when, will, win, winner, with, woke, yelled, yes, you, zoomed

High-Frequency Words

New
even, pushed, studied, surprised, toward

Previously Taught
a, by, could, give, I, I'll, said, the, they, was, would

The Three Races

page 32

Decodable Words

Target Skill: Inflections *-er*, *-est*
bigger, faster, slower, speedier, nicer, fatter

Previously Taught Skills
and, at, be, black, blue, box, cars, chose, each, fast, first, Fran, Fran's, green, had, happy, her, hill, hoped, in, it, Ken, Ken's, last, lined, made, much, next, not, racecars, picked, race, raced, races, red, same, she, slick, speed, speedy, stripes, than, that, them, then, this, time, too, top, up, wheels, which, win, with, zipped, zoomed

High-Frequency Words

New
enough, happy

Previously Taught
a, of, one, the, to, two, was, would

Seed Sisters

page 42

Decodable Words

Target Skill: Inflections *-er, -est*
bigger, faster, flatter, higher, longer,
nicest, quicker, rounder, shorter, slower

Previously Taught Skills
and, as, back, backyard, bloom, buds,
day, dig, digs, each, first, for, from,
go, got, grow, her, home, how, in, is,
it, just, last, Liz, Liz's, longer, looks,
much, nice, pack, picks, plant, plants,
plot, rake, Rose, Rose's, rounder, see,
seed, seeds, shopping, spring, sprout,
stories, tell, than, that, think, town,
wait, weed, yard

High-Frequency Words

New
always, different, high,
higher, once, stories

Previously Taught
a, are, of, smaller, the, their,
they, to

Jingle, Jangle, and Jiggle

page 52

Decodable Words

Target Skill: Syllable -_le
chuckle, dangles, giggle, grumble, Jangle, Jangle's, Jiggle, Jiggle's, Jingle, Jingle's, middle, mumbles, puzzle, sniffles, tackles

Target Skill: Inflections *-er, -est*
biggest, longest, loudest, shortest, silliest

Previously Taught Skills
and, back, be, beak, bird, bird's, blue, boots, bow, box, can, cannot, catch, clown, clowns, dips, dress, from, funny, get, happy, has, hat, hats, he, his, honk, honking, inside, is, it, in, jumps, looks, loud, low, make, makes, missing, must, names, need, nose, noses, not, now, on, pals, pants, places, popcorn, see, silly, starts, still, snatches, sobs, sound, take, that, then, up, us, zooms

High-Frequency Words

New
always, high, near

Previously Taught
a, are, comes, does, gives, I, my, put, puts, the, they, to, where

Accompanies *"The Kite"*

Sally Jane and Beth Ann

page 62

Decodable Words

Target Skill: Long *i* Spelling Patterns
igh, y, ie
bright, by, cried, flight, fly, high, my,
night, sighed, sky, tight, try

Previously Taught Skills

am, an, and, Ann, at, back, bat, best,
Beth, bit, boasted, brown, buddy,
bugs, can, can't, catch, cave, dark, far,
feet, flew, free, from, gave, get, go,
good, got, grasp, groaned, hanging,
happy, held, help, helped, her, in, is, it,
Jane, landed, last, let, let's, lift, liked,
me, much, needed, net, new, odd,
out, pick, safe, Sally, saw, she, smile,
snagged, so, sound, sounds, spent,
stiff, still, strong, thanked, that, then,
this, time, took, tugged, up, will, wing,
with, you

High-Frequency Words

New
across, cried, heard, large

Previously Taught

a, away, could, hear,
hearing, I, of, said, the, they,
to, was, what

Ty and Big Gilly

Decodable Words
Target Skill: Long *i* Spelling Patterns
igh, y, ie
by, bright, cried, fighting, fly, high, right, sight, sky, tried, try, Ty

Previously Taught Skills
and, as, at, back, baited, bed, best, big, biggest, bite, blue, box, bug, bugs, cast, clean, closed, dad, day, filled, fish, fishing, forth, gave, Gilly, glad, go, grabbed, had, happy, hard, he, head, hiked, him, his, hobby, hook, hooks, in, it, its, jelly, jumped, keep, kept, king, lake, landed, large, let, lid, liked, line, made, neat, off, on, out, pale, plop, reel, rod, sand, sat, sorts, snapped, still, stuff, sunny, swam, tail, that, that's, then, threw, time, took, under, up, used, waited, went, winked, with

High-Frequency Words
New
across, cried, head, large, second

Previously Taught
a, all, also, of, one, the, to, was, water, what

Benches

Decodable Words
Target Skill: Inflections *-s, -es, -ed, -ing*

Target Skill: beaches, benches, books, buddies, cities, comics, couches, dads, dogs, funnies, games, grown-ups, kids, leashes, likes, lunchboxes, moms, parks, pets, places, playing, puppies, rains, reading, resting, sitting, streets, towns, winners, yards

Target Skill: Long *i* Spelling Patterns *igh, y, ie*
by, bright, might, sight, sky

Previously Taught Skills
and, at, but, can, chat, dad, eat, flow, for, go, good, in, is, it, jump, like, lunchtime, me, not, on, or, out, outside, play, read, rest, rope, sea, see, side, sit, still, sunny, them, then, this, too, when, win, you, zoo

High-Frequency Words
New
ball, should

Previously Taught
a, are, don't, have, many, over, some, the, they, to, watch, what

Quiz Game

page 92

Decodable Words
Target Skill: Suffixes *-ful*, *-ly*, *-y*
furry, helpful, hopeful, icy, loudly,
quickly, softly, slowly, spotty, squeaky,
stinky, sweetly

Previously Taught Skills
be, big, biggest, bird, black, book,
bright, by, can, cat, claws, did, dog,
each, fast, feathers, fish, five, fly, for,
fun, game, go, growl, has, hump, in, is,
it, leap, legs, like, long, looks, lot, make,
more, new, on, page, path, purr, quick,
quiz, running, shell, sing, six, snake,
sound, stripes, swim, than, that, this,
three, which, white, wiggle, will, you,
you'll, zigzag, zip

High-Frequency Words
New
any, hello, ideas

Previously Taught
a, animal, animals, are, do,
have, I, I'm, the, was, water

Jack and the Beans

page 102

Decodable Words

Target Skill: Suffixes *-ful*, *-ly*, *-y*
bagful, cupful, gladly, handful, hopeful,
hopefully, joyful, quickly, thankful

Previously Taught Skills

after, an, and, as, at, ate, back, bean,
beans, big, black, but, came, cow, did,
down, drenched, dry, dug, fat, feed,
feel, felt, fetch, food, for, get, good, got,
green, grew, had, happy, he, helped,
hill, his, it, Jack, Jack's, Jill, land, last,
liked, long, looked, lot, much, nice, not,
oatmeal, pail, picked, plan, planted,
plants, plot, rakes, rows, see, sell,
she, silly, soil, soon, spades, sprouted,
sprouts, still, such, that, them, then,
those, took, town, time, traded, up,
upset, waited, went, with

High-Frequency Words

New
gone, idea

Previously Taught
a, could, have, of, one,
some, the, their, to, was,
were, would

Stew for Peg

page 112

Decodable Words

Target Skill: Long Vowel Spelling
Patterns: *a, e, i, o, u*
able, be, cozy, he, hi, Hugo, I, Jo, Lulu,
she, Toby

Target Skill: Suffixes *-ful, -ly, -y*
cupful, handful, helpful, loudly, quickly,
really, yummy

Previously Taught Skills
ask, asked, back, big, birthday, cart,
chattered, did, didn't, for, green, had,
happened, happy, heat, help, helped,
her, home, hot, hooted, how, in, is,
it, it's, know, leaves, likes, make, not,
on, Owl, own, Peg, Peg's, Pig's, pot,
quacked, red, sat, smells, squealed,
stew, stuff, such, thanks, that, this, treat,
up, went, will, with, you

High-Frequency Words

New
happened, leaves

Previously Taught
a, all, of, put, said, some,
there, to, wanted, was,
water, what

Amy Ant

page 122

Decodable Words

Target Skill: Syllable Pattern (CV)
able, Amy, before, cozy, decides, music, over, reminds, returns, Rupert, tiger

Previously Taught Skills

after, and, Ant, as, at, back, backpack, be, bed, better, blooming, blue, brave, crawls, day, days, did, down, each, ending, feels, field, fills, flies, flowers, flying, for, fun, get, go, good, had, happy, has, he, help, her, him, his, home, how, hums, is, it, its, last, leave, long, look, makes, mantis, meet, most, name, next, not, now, on, out, pick, room, roses, sad, saves, see, sees, shouts, smell, sleepy, slides, slips, sniffs, so, soon, spring, summer, sunny, sunshine, take, tells, thanks, that, time, too, tune, up, way, wakes, waves, when, will, winter

High-Frequency Words

New
field, loves, most

Previously Taught
a, are, been, come, every, full, have, hears, into, of, one, some, talk, the, they, to, walks, you're

LESSON 30

Julie and Jason

page 132

Decodable Words

Target Skill: Syllable Pattern (CV)
able, baby, before, behave, behind,
believe, beyond, cozy, even, Jason, Julie,
Julie's, over, silent, table

Previously Taught Skills

after, an, and, as, asked, back, big, black,
by, can, cat, curls, day, did, dinner, dog,
drapes, each, eats, feeds, find, for, fur,
game, got, had, happy, has, hay, he,
her, hidden, hide, hides, him, his, hop,
hopped, house, hunts, hutch, if, in,
it, lap, let, like, likes, looked, missing,
named, no, not, off, on, or, out, outside,
pellets, pet, picnic, places, plant, play,
playing, porch, rabbit, sad, saw, see,
seek, seeks, seen, she, sit, sits, smiled,
sleeps, so, spotted, still, takes, them,
then, time, too, took, up, upset, when,
white, with

High-Frequency Words

New
brothers, everyone, sorry

Previously Taught
a, all, away, couldn't, idea,
of, was, one, the, their, they,
to, were

176

LESSON 30

Soccer

page 142

Decodable Words
Target Skill: Prefixes *un*, *re*
react, replaying, retelling, unkind, unlike, unsafe, unskilled

Target Skill: Syllable Pattern (CV)
behave, believe, decided, remind

Previously Taught Skills
and, at, be, best, blue, boys, bump, by, can, catch, chose, coach, coach's, dots, dressed, each, ends, fast, feet, field, first, for, from, fun, game, games, get, girls, goal, goalkeeper, goalkeepers, goals, good, has, he, her, his, is, it, job, keep, kick, kids, kind, long, look, made, making, matter, may, more, most, must, need, no, on, or, out, pads, pick, play, plays, player, players, red, safely, same, say, score, she, shin, shirt, shirts, skillful, skills, soccer, socks, sport, stop, stripes, teach, team, teams, team's, telling, these

High-Frequency Words
New
everyone, field, most, only, people

Previously Taught
a, are, ball, have, into, many, of, putting, the, their, they, to, who